MATHS Workbook

Level 3

Published in Moonstone
by Rupa Publications India Pvt. Ltd 2022
7/16, Ansari Road, Daryaganj
New Delhi 110002

Sales centres:
Allahabad Bengaluru Chennai
Hyderabad Jaipur Kathmandu
Kolkata Mumbai

Copyright © Rupa Publications India Pvt. Ltd 2022

The views and opinions expressed in this book are
the authors' own and the facts are as reported by them
which have been verified to the extent possible,
and the publishers are not in any way liable for the same.

All rights reserved.
No part of this publication may be reproduced, transmitted,
or stored in a retrieval system, in any form or by any means,
electronic, mechanical, photocopying, recording or otherwise,
without the prior permission of the publisher.

ISBN: 978-93-5520-720-3

First impression 2022

10 9 8 7 6 5 4 3 2 1

The moral right of the authors has been asserted.

Printed in India
This book is sold subject to the condition that it shall not,
by way of trade or otherwise, be lent, resold, hired out, or otherwise
circulated, without the publisher's prior consent, in any form of binding
or cover other than that in which it is published.

Contents

- Numbers Beyond 1000 4
- Place Value and Face Value 5
- Expanded Form 6
- Roman Numerals 7
- Ordering Numbers 9
- Adding Numbers 12
- Subtracting Numbers 15
- Face the Challenge 17
- Solve the Puzzles 18
- Rounding Off 19
- Estimate and Solve 21
- Multiplication 23
- Division 25
- More Than, Less Than 27
- Fractions 29
- Equivalent Fractions 30
- Ordering Fractions 31
- Adding Fractions 32
- Measuring Length 33
- Money 37
- Geometry 39
- Patterns and Symmetry 41
- Calendar 42
- Time 44
- Data Handling 46
- Answers 47

Numbers Beyond 1000

1. Complete the number grids by filling in the missing numbers.

(a)
1001	1002		1004				1008		1010
1011				1015					1020
1021		1023				1027			
	1032				1036			1039	
			1044				1048		1050

(b)
2081			2084						2090
	2092					2097			2100
2101			2104				2108		
2111		2113			2116			2119	
	2122			2125					2130

(c)
9951				9955					9960
		9963				9967		9969	
	9972				9976				9980
9981				9984				9988	
		9993			9995				10000

Place Value and Face Value

1. Write the place value and face value of the underlined digits.

Number	Place value	Face value
(a) 4<u>6</u>78		
(b) 1<u>9</u>99		
(c) <u>3</u>671		
(d) 62<u>9</u>4		
(e) <u>7</u>742		
(f) 9<u>3</u>27		

Number	Place value	Face value
(g) 732<u>5</u>		
(h) <u>1</u>428		
(i) 8<u>4</u>95		
(j) 5<u>1</u>39		
(k) 22<u>9</u>7		
(l) <u>8</u>926		

2. Make the greatest and smallest 4-digit number using the given digits.

Digits	Greatest 4-digit no.	Smallest 4-digit no.
(a) 4, 3, 7, 2		
(b) 1, 9, 3, 8		
(c) 5, 0, 2, 6		
(d) 8, 4, 0, 2		
(e) 6, 5, 7, 1		
(f) 2, 6, 9, 4		
(g) 7, 8, 3, 5		

Expanded Form

1. Write the following in expanded form as given.

    (a) 7426 = 7000 + 400 + 20 + 6

    (b) 3908 = _____

    (c) 1524 = _____

    (d) 6330 = _____

    (e) 4513 = _____

    (f) 9999 = _____

2. Expand the following numbers as given.

    (a) 3284 = 3 × 1000 + 2 × 100 + 8 × 10 + 4 × 1

    (b) 8047 = _____

    (c) 9551 = _____

    (d) 6382 = _____

    (e) 1499 = _____

    (f) 7107 = _____

    (g) 2965 = _____

    (h) 6834 = _____

Roman Numerals

1. Write the Roman numerals for the following.

(a) 7		(i) 6		(q) 16	
(b) 2		(j) 10		(r) 13	
(c) 8		(k) 20		(s) 70	
(d) 3		(l) 50		(t) 60	
(e) 5		(m) 29		(u) 100	
(f) 9		(n) 15		(v) 300	
(g) 4		(o) 18		(w) 500	
(h) 1		(p) 12		(x) 1000	

2. Write the Hindu-Arabic numerals for each of the following.

(a) X		(i) XXI		(q) XXXV	
(b) IV		(j) XIV		(r) LX	
(c) VII		(k) XXX		(s) L	
(d) III		(l) XV		(t) CC	
(e) IX		(m) XVII		(u) XL	
(f) V		(n) XII		(v) D	
(g) VIII		(o) XIX		(w) DCC	
(h) II		(p) XVIII		(x) M	

3. Answer the following in Roman numerals.

(a) I am _____ years old.

(b) I study in class _____.

(c) There are _____ children in my class.

(d) I have _____ books in my bag.

(e) There are _____ people in my house.

(f) I have _____ fingers on my hands.

(g) 16 + 4 = <u>20</u> = <u>XX</u>

(h) 200 + 300 = _____ = _____

(i) 50 + 150 = _____ = _____

(j) 164 + 336 = _____ = _____

(k) 1000 − 400 = _____ = _____

(l) 85 + 15 = _____ = _____

(m) 350 − 250 = _____ = _____

(n) 57 − 48 = _____ = _____

(o) 6 × 3 = _____ = _____

(p) 25 × 4 = _____ = _____

(q) 100 × 10 = _____ = _____

(r) 56 ÷ 8 = _____ = _____

(s) 60 ÷ 12 = _____ = _____

(t) 1000 ÷ 25 = _____ = _____

Ordering Numbers

1. Arrange each of the following in the ascending order.

   (a) 3154, 4295, 2160, 1740 _____

   (b) 1045, 1005, 1645, 1405 _____

   (c) 634, 6342, 6213, 6142 _____

   (d) 7842, 4509, 1634, 5204 _____

   (e) 4976, 2908, 453, 924 _____

2. Arrange each of the following in the descending order.

   (a) 1864, 7104, 8192, 4521 _____

   (b) 432, 2727, 6121, 812 _____

   (c) 3541, 6145, 4152, 5161 _____

   (d) 732, 1632, 2732, 632 _____

   (e) 2069, 6029, 9026, 629 _____

3. Use the digits given in column A to make any 4 different 4-digit numbers.

Column A	4-digit numbers			
(a) 4, 3, 6, 1				
(b) 7, 9, 2, 4				
(c) 3, 5, 8, 0				
(d) 1, 6, 7, 9				
(e) 8, 4, 1, 3				
(f) 2, 9, 6, 0				
(g) 5, 0, 7, 1				
(h) 4, 3, 9, 2				

4. **Write the odd numbers from 1 to 17 in the given circles so that the sum of each side of the triangle is 30. Each number can be used only once. Three numbers have already been placed.**

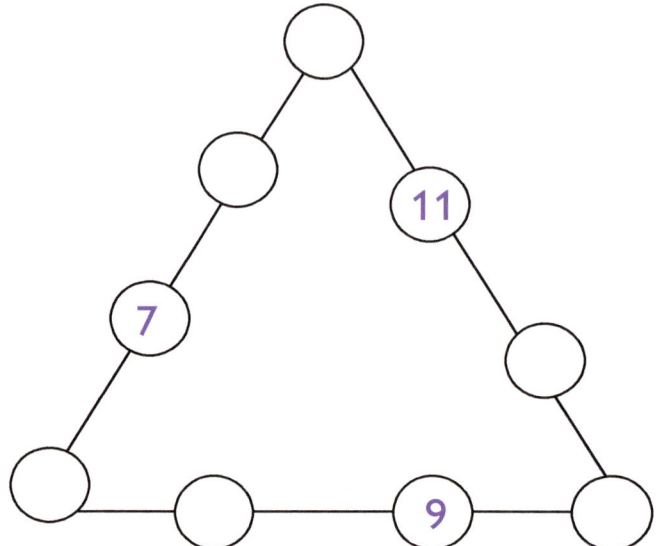

1, 3, 5, 7̶, 9̶, 1̶1̶, 13, 15, 17

5. **Fill in the blanks with the correct numbers.**

(a) The smallest 4-digit number is _____.

(b) The predecessor of the smallest 4-digit number is _____.

(c) The successor of the largest 3-digit number is _____.

(d) The smallest number formed by using the digits 4, 9, 6, 3, is _____.

(e) The Roman numeral for the successor of the largest 2-digit number is _____.

(f) The difference between the largest and smallest 3-digit number is _____.

(g) The Roman numeral for the largest 1-digit number is _____.

(h) The place value of 9 in 4927 is _____.

(i) The face value of 6 in 2968 is _____.

(j) The difference between the place value and face value of 3 in 4630 is _____.

6. Write all the even numbers between 4625 and 4657.

_____

_____

_____

_____

7. Write all the odd numbers which come between 7410 and 7460.

_____

_____

_____

_____

8. Write the predecessor and sucessor for the following numbers.

	Predecessor	Number	Successor
(a)		3429	
(b)		1986	
(c)		4200	
(d)		5861	
(e)		2999	
(f)		4601	

Adding Numbers

A. Use the properties of addition to fill in the blanks.

1. 1040 + 2080 = _____ + 1040

2. 2375 + 625 = _____ + 0

3. 0 + 4998 = _____

4. (600 + 425) + 1425 = _____ + (1425 + 600)

5. (173 + 900) + 781 = _____ + (900 + 781)

6. 5000 + _____ = 5001

7. 3999 + _____ = 4000

8. 4829 + 1000 = _____

9. 1240 + 700 = _____

10. 6420 + 2000 = _____

B. Read the statements and write the sum.

1. 5 hundreds + 4 tens + 8 ones = _____

2. 8 thousands + 8 hundreds + 5 tens + 5 ones = _____

3. 4 thousands + 6 hundreds + 3 ones = _____

4. 6 thousands + 7 tens + 2 ones = _____

5. 2 hundreds + 9 tens + 7 ones = _____

C. Write the number which doubles up and makes the given sum for each of the following.

1.	_____ + _____ = 50	2.	_____ + _____ = 100
3.	_____ + _____ = 1000	4.	_____ + _____ = 2000
5.	_____ + _____ = 700	6.	_____ + _____ = 8000
7.	_____ + _____ = 6000	8.	_____ + _____ = 500
9.	_____ + _____ = 10	10.	_____ + _____ = 9000

D. Arrange the numbers in columns and add them.

1. 6719 + 1275

2. 4868 + 3570

3. 7558 + 1234

4. 4299 + 2715

5. 5788 + 3542

6. 2756 + 6185

E. Solve the following word problems.

Working Space

1. There are 4624 men and 3926 women in a village. If there are 624 children also, what is the total population of the village?

   Answer: _____

2. Mandy travels 2840 km distance by train and 1642 km distance by bus to reach her house. What is the total distance travelled by her?

   Answer: _____

3. A fruit seller sold 5426 kg fruits in one month and 4059 kg fruits in the next month. How many kgs of fruits did he sell?

   Answer: _____

4. Mrs. Smith bought a mobile phone for $2920 and a school kit for $1458. How much money should she pay to the shopkeeper?

   Answer: _____

5. A worker is carrying a bag of rice weighing 2500 kg and a bag of cereals weighing 1500 kg. How much weight is he carrying?

   Answer: _____

6. Tina tied two ropes of length 5425 m and 3648 m together. What is the total length of the rope now?

   Answer: _____

Subtracting Numbers

A. Arrange the numbers in columns and subtract.

1. 4628 from 9399

2. 3475 from 7969

3. 2908 from 6423

4. 6694 from 9000

5. 1045 from 7820

6. 3268 from 5468

7. 3005 from 8645

8. 2309 from 5497

9. 4400 from 5097

10. 3811 from 6521

B. Solve the following word problems.

Working Space

1. There are 1425 seats in a cinema hall. If 942 are already occupied, how many more people can sit?

   Answer: _____

2. A man buys a TV for $2860 and sells it for $3000. How much money did he earn?

   Answer: _____

3. A rope was 2500 m long. If a part measuring 1220 m was cut out, what is the length of the rope that is left?

   Answer: _____

4. A lady baked 908 buns in a week but could sell only 852 of them. How many buns are left with her now?

   Answer: _____

5. What is the difference between the largest 4-digit number and the smallest 4-digit number?

   Answer: _____

6. In a 3500 m race, a boy runs for 1288 m. How much distance is still left for him to cover?

   Answer: _____

Face the Challenge

A. Choose the correct option for each of the following.

1. Which of the following has 4610 as the answer?
   (a) 3160 + 1000   (b) 4000 + 610   (c) 4010 + 610

2. Which of the following has 2800 as the answer?
   (a) 3000 − 800   (b) 4000 − 200   (c) 2900 − 100

3. The difference between 429 × 10 and 400 × 10 is _____
   (a) 290   (b) 29   (c) 2900

4. Which two numbers can be added to get 1000?
   (a) 500 and 900   (b) 800 and 200   (c) 700 and 400

5. Find the odd statement.
   (a) 600 + 423 = 423 + 600
   (b) 840 + 160 = 160 + 840
   (c) 375 + 608 = 675 + 308

6. Which pair has numbers with same place value of 7?
   (a) 2307, 1476   (b) 427, 7428   (c) 1475, 278

7. Find the wrong statement.
   (a) 296 + (148 + 250) = 250 + (296 + 150)
   (b) 423 + (500 + 714) = 500 + (714 + 423)
   (c) 800 + (745 + 281) = 281 + (800 + 745)

Solve the Puzzles

A. Use number operations to solve the puzzles given below.

3	+	5	=	
+		+		+
	+	15	=	30
=		=		=
18	+		=	

20	+		=	38
+		+		+
12	+	12	=	
=		=		=
	+	30	=	

B. Use multiplication to solve the given puzzles.

1.
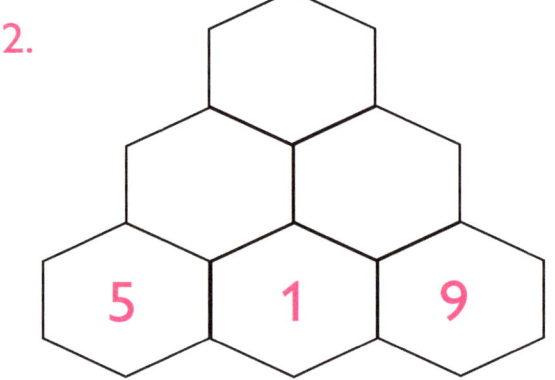

2.

3.
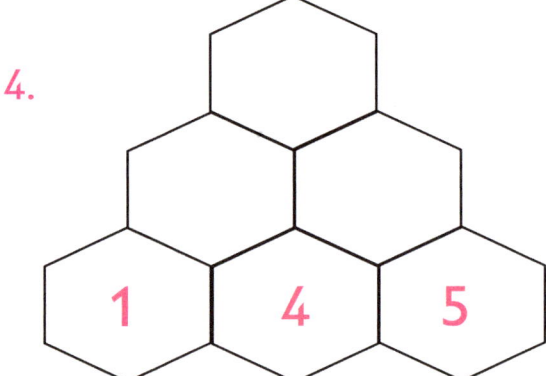

4.

Rounding Off

A. Round off the numbers to the nearest 10.

1. 57 _____
2. 21 _____
3. 84 _____
4. 32 _____
5. 71 _____

6. 39 _____
7. 76 _____
8. 68 _____
9. 29 _____
10. 48 _____

11. 42 _____
12. 13 _____
13. 57 _____
14. 75 _____
15. 94 _____

B. Round off the numbers to the nearest 100.

1. 876 _____
2. 249 _____
3. 683 _____
4. 420 _____
5. 755 _____
6. 267 _____

7. 198 _____
8. 361 _____
9. 527 _____
10. 915 _____
11. 150 _____
12. 446 _____

13. 3671 _____
14. 4238 _____
15. 6990 _____
16. 7365 _____
17. 1949 _____
18. 8259 _____

C. Round off the numbers to the nearest 1000.

1. 6248 _____
2. 3928 _____
3. 4559 _____
4. 1111 _____
5. 8692 _____

6. 2831 _____
7. 5064 _____
8. 1792 _____
9. 9321 _____
10. 7457 _____

D. Round off the numbers to the nearest 10 and 100.

Numbers	Nearest 10	Nearest 100
1. 478		
2. 923		
3. 1562		
4. 270		
5. 847		
6. 669		

Estimate and Solve

A. Estimate the sum by rounding each number to the nearest 100. Compare the estimated sum with the correct answer. See the example given below.

①
```
   3 6 9  →    4 0 0         2 4 8
+  1 2 3  → +  1 0 0      +  6 9 3
  -------     -------        -------
   4 9 2       5 0 0
```

```
   1 0 1                     3 0 1
+  7 6 3                  +  4 7 2
```

```
   3 8 8                     7 9 2
+  9 0 9                  +  5 2 1
```

```
   2 1 0                     6 2 8
+  8 2 4                  +  4 5 1
```

```
   4 8 8                     5 1 2
+  3 0 5                  +  1 8 9
```

B. Estimate the difference by rounding each number to the nearest 100. Compare the estimated difference with the correct answer. See the example given below.

739 → 700 − 478 → − 500 ───────────── 261 200	826 − 819 ────────
667 − 144 ────────	717 − 507 ────────
936 − 474 ────────	542 − 356 ────────
489 − 377 ────────	898 − 517 ────────
620 − 456 ────────	880 − 260 ────────

Multiplication

A. Multiply the numbers and fill in the blanks.

1. 5 × 10 = _____

2. 12 × 5 = _____ = 6 × _____

3. 18 × 100 = _____ × 10

4. 28 × 2 = _____

5. 25 × 4 = _____ = 10 × _____

6. 164 × 10 = _____

7. 12800 = 128 × _____

8. 1600 = 16 × _____ = 4 × _____ × 100

B. Arrange the numbers in columns and multiply.

1. 4 2 3 by 2	2. 2 6 4 by 5
3. 1 5 7 by 4	4. 3 5 8 by 3

C. Read the word problems and solve them.

1. You have 11 bags with 8 hats in each bag. How many hats do you have in all?

   Answer: _____

2. Ben writes 24 pages of his handwriting book daily for a week. How many pages has he written in all?

   Answer: _____

3. A baker decorates each cake with 9 cherries. If she bakes 32 cakes, how many cherries will she need?

   Answer: _____

4. Sam went to watch a puppet show. Each puppet was connected with 4 strings. If 57 different puppets were used in the show, how many strings would be used?

   Answer: _____

5. The ticket for a stage show costs $125. How much will 6 tickets cost?

   Answer: _____

6. There are 49 spiders in a web. How many legs are there in all?

   Answer: _____

Division

A. Divide the numbers and fill in the blanks.

1. 460 ÷ 10 = _____
2. 81 ÷ 9 = _____
3. 20 ÷ 2 = _____ = _____ × 2
4. 500 ÷ 100 = _____ = 5 × _____
5. 250 ÷ 5 = _____
6. 32 ÷ 8 = _____
7. 990 ÷ 11 = _____
8. 70 ÷ 7 = _____
9. 8700 ÷ 100 = _____
10. 4300 ÷ 10 = _____

B. Arrange the numbers in brackets and divide. Also write the quotient and the remainder.

1. Divide 45 by 5.

   Q = ☐
   R = ☐

2. Divide 36 by 2.

   Q = ☐
   R = ☐

3. Divide 74 by 3.

Q = ☐
R = ☐

4. Divide 48 by 4.

Q = ☐
R = ☐

5. Divide 50 by 2.

Q = ☐
R = ☐

6. Divide 36 by 3.

Q = ☐
R = ☐

7. Divide 46 by 3.

Q = ☐
R = ☐

8. Divide 39 by 4.

Q = ☐
R = ☐

More Than, Less Than

A. Read the statements and write the correct answer.

1. 45 more than 39 is _____.

2. 37 less than 100 is _____.

3. 64 less than the largest 2-digit number is _____.

4. 23 more than the largest 2-digit number is _____.

5. 97 more than 100 is _____.

6. 46 less than 256 is _____.

7. 29 less than 50 is _____.

8. 60 more than 20 is _____.

9. 52 less than 70 is _____.

10. 48 more than 12 is _____.

11. 10 more than the smallest even number is _____.

12. 50 more than the smallest odd number is _____.

13. 25 less than 100 is _____.

14. 1 less than the smallest even number is _____.

B. Complete the table given below.

	50 less than	Number	50 more than
1.		1648	
2.		7394	
3.		4260	
4.		7518	
5.		1982	
6.		5551	
7.		3726	

C. Complete the table given below.

	500 less than	Number	500 more than
1.		6285	
2.		1900	
3.		5488	
4.		7231	
5.		2660	
6.		8500	
7.		4758	

Fractions

A. Shade the shapes according to the given fractions.

1.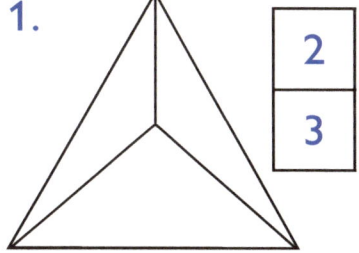
2.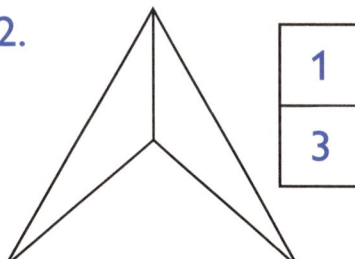
3.

4.
5.
6.

7.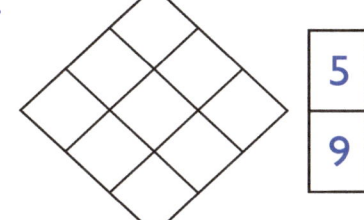
8.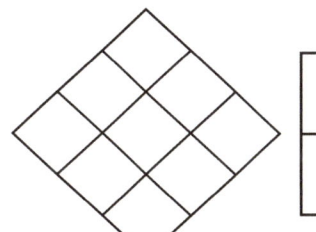
9.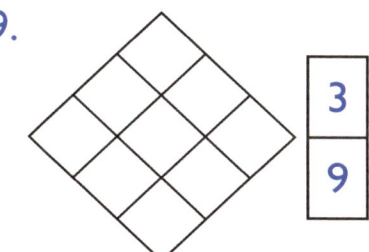

B. Write the fractions for the shaded parts of the whole.

1.
2.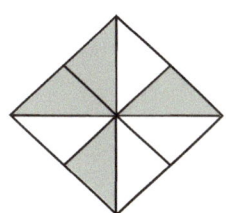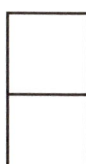

3.
4.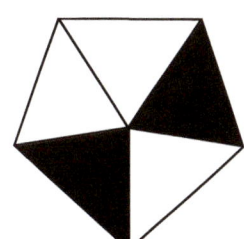

Equivalent Fractions

A. Write the fractions for the shaded parts of whole and write the equivalent fraction for each.

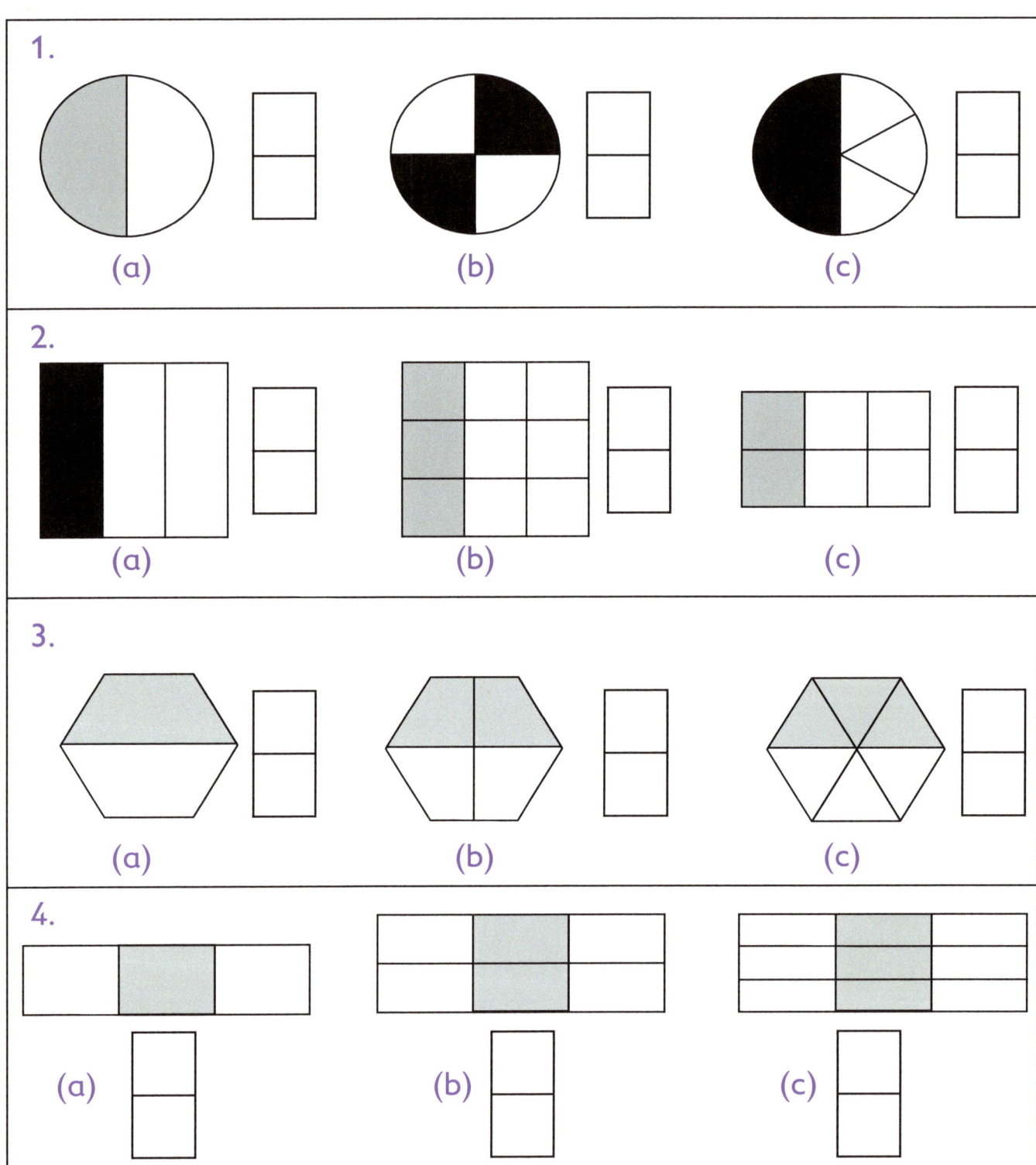

Ordering Fractions

A. Arrange the fractions in the correct order.

(1) $\dfrac{5}{9}$, $\dfrac{6}{9}$, $\dfrac{1}{9}$, $\dfrac{4}{9}$, $\dfrac{3}{9}$, $\dfrac{7}{9}$

☐ > ☐ > ☐ > ☐ > ☐ > ☐

(2) $\dfrac{2}{7}$, $\dfrac{6}{7}$, $\dfrac{4}{7}$, $\dfrac{5}{7}$, $\dfrac{1}{7}$, $\dfrac{7}{7}$

☐ < ☐ < ☐ < ☐ < ☐ < ☐

(3) $\dfrac{1}{6}$, $\dfrac{4}{6}$, $\dfrac{3}{6}$, $\dfrac{5}{6}$, $\dfrac{2}{6}$, 1

☐ > ☐ > ☐ > ☐ > ☐ > ☐

(4) $\dfrac{3}{8}$, $\dfrac{5}{8}$, $\dfrac{4}{8}$, $\dfrac{6}{8}$, $\dfrac{2}{8}$, $\dfrac{7}{8}$

☐ < ☐ < ☐ < ☐ < ☐ < ☐

(5) $\dfrac{9}{12}$, $\dfrac{3}{12}$, $\dfrac{5}{12}$, $\dfrac{11}{12}$, $\dfrac{1}{12}$, $\dfrac{7}{12}$

☐ > ☐ > ☐ > ☐ > ☐ > ☐

Adding Fractions

A. Shade the part of whole shapes to add the fractions.
   See the example given below and find the sum of others.

1. 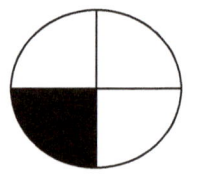 +  =

   $\dfrac{1}{4}$ + $\dfrac{2}{4}$ = $\dfrac{3}{4}$

2. 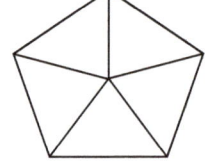 + 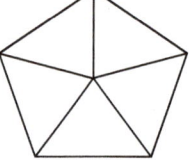 =

   $\dfrac{2}{5}$ + $\dfrac{2}{5}$ = ☐

3. 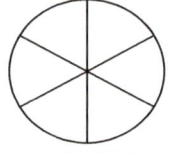 +  =

   $\dfrac{1}{6}$ + $\dfrac{3}{6}$ = ☐

4.  + 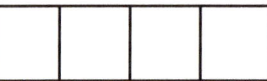 =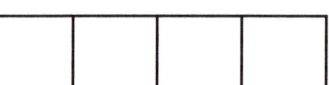

   $\dfrac{1}{4}$ + $\dfrac{3}{4}$ = ☐

5. 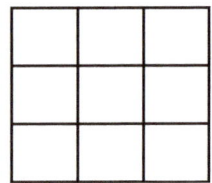 + 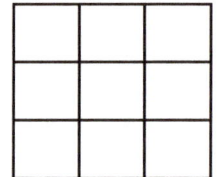 =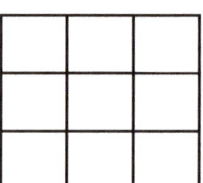

   $\dfrac{4}{9}$ + $\dfrac{2}{9}$ = ☐

Measuring Length

A. Convert each of the following into centimetres (cm).

1. 1 m = _____ cm
2. 4 m = _____ cm
3. 7 m = _____ cm
4. 3 m = _____ cm
5. 9 m = _____ cm
6. 8 m = _____ cm
7. 12 m = _____ cm
8. 6 m = _____ cm
9. 15 m = _____ cm
10. 5 m = _____ cm

B. Convert each of the following into metres (m).

1. 100 cm = _____ m
2. 300 cm = _____ m
3. 800 cm = _____ m
4. 200 cm = _____ m
5. 1100 cm = _____ m
6. 600 cm = _____ m
7. 700 cm = _____ m
8. 1400 cm = _____ m
9. 1 km = _____ m
10. 9 km = _____ m
11. 7 km = _____ m
12. 3 km = _____ m

C. Convert each of the following into centimetres (cm).

1. 6 m 5 cm = _____ cm
2. 2 m 20 cm = _____ cm
3. 9 m 10 cm = _____ cm
4. 5 m 8 cm = _____ cm
5. 12 m 12 cm = _____ cm
6. 3 m 42 cm = _____ cm
7. 8 m 88 cm = _____ cm
8. 1 m 56 cm = _____ cm
9. 15 m 68 cm = _____ cm
10. 10 m 38 cm = _____ cm

D. Tick the most suitable answer for each of the following.

1. The length of the writing board in your class.

    (a) 2 cm	(b) 2 m	(c) 2 km

2. The length of a pencil.

    (a) 10 cm	(b) 10 m	(c) 10 km

3. The length of a river.

    (a) 50 cm	(b) 5 m	(c) 50 km

4. The length of an eraser.

    (a) 3 cm	(b) 3 m	(c) 3 km

5. The length of a table cloth.

    (a) 1 cm	(b) 1 m	(c) 1 km

E. Solve the given problems and write the answer.

1.
m	cm
73	14
+ 25	87

2.
m	cm
36	28
+ 25	42

3.
m	cm
75	19
− 25	34

4.
km	m
84	256
− 32	175

5.
km	m
32	78
+ 46	24

6.
km	m
43	175
− 26	139

F. Fill in the blanks given below.

1. 1 km = _____ m = 500 m + _____ m
2. 1 kg = _____ g = 500 g + _____ g
3. 5 kg = _____ g = 4000 g + _____ g
4. 1 l = _____ ml = 900 ml + _____ ml
5. 1 km = _____ m = 400 m + _____ m
6. 1 l = _____ ml = 200 ml + _____ ml
7. 9 m = _____ cm = 300 cm + _____ cm
8. 12 km = _____ m = 2000 m + _____ m
9. 10 l = _____ ml = 5 l + _____ l
10. 7 kg = _____ g = 10 kg – _____ kg
11. 12 m = _____ cm = 10 m + _____ m
12. 18 l = _____ ml = 20 l – _____ l

G. Write the correct measurement unit for each of the following (m, l, kg):

1. Weight of a bag full of rice. _____
2. Length of a cloth. _____
3. Volume of a can of milk. _____
4. Quantity of water in a jug. _____
5. Quantity of wheat in a sack. _____
6. Height of a wall. _____
7. Distance covered by you to reach school. _____
8. Weight of vegetables in a basket. _____

H. Solve the word problems given below.

Working Space

1. The length of a red ribbon is 54 m and that of a blue ribbon is 38 m. Which ribbon is longer and by how much?

    Answer: _____

2. A milkman is carrying two cans with quantity 25 l and 1500 ml respectively. How much quantity of milk is he carrying in all?

    Answer: _____

3. Tiya has a 4 m 36 cm long lace. She wants to know the length of the lace in centimetres. Calculate the answer for her.

    Answer: _____

4. Jimmy has 9 pencils of the same type. Each of them measures 13 cm. If he puts them in a straight row, what will be the length of the row?

    Answer: _____

5. The quantity of a glass is 50 ml. If a man drinks twenty glasses of water from the same glass, how much water did he drink in all?

    Answer: _____

6. Siya has 8 bags of cereals measuring 780 gm each. How much weight does she have in all?

    Answer: _____

Money

A. Convert each of the following into cents.

1. $1 = _____ cents
2. $8 = _____ cents
3. $3 = _____ cents
4. $6 and 15 cents = _____ cents
5. $10 and 25 cents = _____ cents
6. $5 = _____ cents

B. Express the currency values in words.

1. $13.50 _____
2. $10 _____
3. $41.25 _____
4. $0.99 _____
5. $8.18 _____

C. Fill in the blanks with the correct answer from the box given below.

| $56.31 | $105 | 345 cents | $110.25 | cents | $3.60 |

1. $3.45 can also be written as _____.
2. 360 cents can also be written as _____.
3. Sum of $42.80 and $13.51 is _____.
4. A bag costs $12.25. The cost of 9 such bags will be _____.
5. One dollar is equal to 100 _____.
6. The cost of five tickets of a concert is $525. What is the cost of one ticket? _____

D. Solve the word problems to find the answer.

Working Space

1. Renu has two piggy banks with her. One has $124.50 and the other has $384.86. How much money does she have in all?

    Answer: _____

2. A lady bought seven packets of cereals for $36 each. If she paid $1000 to the shopkeeper, how much change did she get back?

    Answer: _____

3. Nitin has $428.50 in his pocket. If he gave $152 to his mother, how much money is left with him?

    Answer: _____

4. Mother divided $546 equally among seven kids. How much money will each kid have?

    Answer: _____

5. A man deposited $185 in his bank account every week. How much money can he save in 2 months by following this habit?

    Answer: _____

Geometry

A. Fill in the blanks with the correct word from the box given below.

| point | two | no | one | definite | ray |

1. A ray has _____ end point.

2. A line has _____ end points.

3. A line segment has _____ end points.

4. A _____ shows a definite position.

5. A line segment has a _____ length.

6. A _____ has one initial point.

B. Draw two points in the given space. Draw as many straight lines passing through both the points as you can.

C. Draw a line segment in the given space that measures 8 cm.

D. Match each solid shape to its correct description.

Solid shapes   **Description**

1. Cuboid   (a) One flat face and one curved face.

2. Cube   (b) Two flat circle faces and one curved face.

3. Sphere   (c) 6 flat faces of the same size.

4. Cone   (d) Only one curved face.

5. Cylinder   (e) 6 flat rectangular faces.

E. Name the closed figure which can be formed by joining:

1. 3 straight lines of the same length _____.

2. 6 straight lines of the same length _____.

3. 4 straight lines of the same length _____.

4. 5 straight lines of the same length _____.

F. Fill in the blanks with the correct word from the box given below.

| flat | vertex | closed | curved | congruent | open |

1. Edges of a solid shape meet at a _____.

2. Figures with the same size and shape are called _____ figures.

3. Figures with different starting and ending points are called _____ figures.

4. Figures which start and end at the same point are called _____ figures.

5. Solids can have _____ or _____ surface.

40

Patterns and Symmetry

A. Draw the line of symmetry for the following figures.

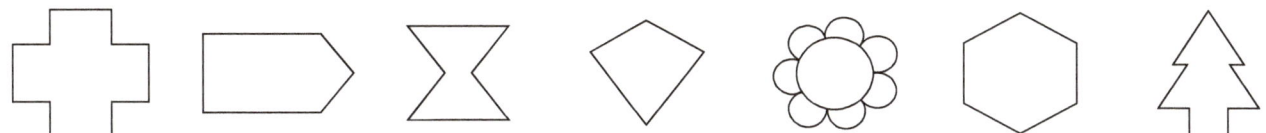

B. Draw the other half of the following figures so that they are symmetrical. Assume that the dotted line is the line of symmetry.

C. Circle the patterns which can be used for tiling.

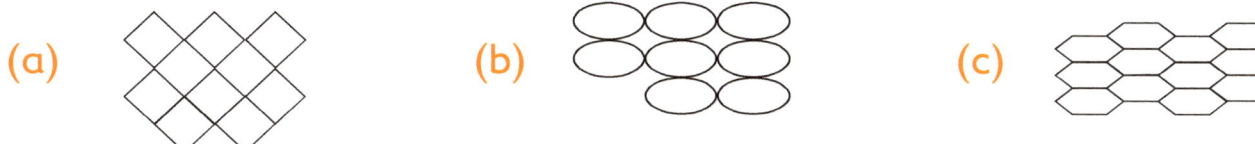

Calendar

A. Use the name of the month to write the dates.

1. 17-03-2008 _____
2. 25-12-2003 _____
3. 04-07-2015 _____
4. 29-02-2000 _____
5. 13-08-2002 _____

B. Write the following dates in numerals.

1. September 5, 2016 _____
2. March 29, 2001 _____
3. August 31, 2014 _____
4. February 18, 2005 _____
5. January 12, 2009 _____

C. Fill in the blanks with the correct answer.

1. A year has _____ months. (twelve/four)
2. Every fourth year is a _____ year. (normal/leap)
3. There are _____ days in a leap year. (365/366)
4. In a leap year, the month of _____ has an extra day. (March/February)
5. There are 31 days in the month of _____. (August/September)
6. A year has _____ weeks. (52/12)

D. Read the calendar of the current year and answer the questions given below.

1. On which day of the week does the month of January start? _____

2. On which day of the week does the month of January end? _____

3. Does any month have 5 Sundays? If yes, name them. _____

4. Write the name of the current month. _____

5. Write today's date. _____

6. How many days are there from May to July? _____

7. How many days are there from 5 August to 19 September? (Include both the dates) _____

8. How many days are there in the current year? _____

9. What is the date after 21 days from today? _____

10. On which day of the week is the first day of the next year? _____

Time

A. Draw the face of clock and show the given time.

Half past 8	Quarter to 6	Quarter past 9
20 minutes past 3	Quarter past 12	10 minutes to 7

B. Write the time for the following. One has been done for you.

1. 8:30 in the morning   _____8:30 am_____

2. 5:15 in the evening   _____

3. 12:38 in the afternoon   _____

4. 11:45 at night   _____

5. 6:21 in the morning   _____

6. 6:12 in the evening   _____

C. Calculate the minutes for each of the following.

1. 2 hours _____
2. 7 hours _____
3. 1 hour 15 minutes _____
4. 1 hour _____
5. 5 hours _____
6. 3 hours 30 minutes _____

D. Calculate the hours for each of the following.

1. 1 day _____
2. 5 days _____
3. 2 days 6 hours _____
4. 60 minutes _____
5. 7 days _____
6. 4 days 3 hours _____

E. Fill in the blanks with the correct answer.

1. 12 o'clock at night is called _____.
2. 12 o'clock in the day is called _____.
3. The long hand of a clock is called the _____.
4. The short hand of a clock is called the _____.
5. If the minute hand is at 6 and the hour hand is between 10 and 11, the time on the clock is _____.
6. 7 o'clock in the morning is written as _____.
7. There are _____ hours in a day.
8. An hour has _____ minutes.
9. You take 5 _____ (minutes/hours) to brush your teeth.
10. We should sleep for at least 8 _____ (minutes/hours).

Data Handling

A. The table given below shows the number of children and their favourite colour. Read the chart carefully and answer the questions given below.

Colour	Number of Students
Blue	15
Grey	4
Yellow	10
Orange	6
Red	12
Pink	11
White	6

1. Which colour is liked by maximum number of students? _____

2. Which colour is liked by least number of students? _____

3. Which two colours are liked by equal number of students? _____, _____

B. The given chart shows the number of books in each child's shelf. Read the chart and answer the questions given below.

Child	Number of Books	= 2 Books
A	7 books	
B	4 books	
C	6 books	
D	8 books	
E	3 books	
F	9 books	
G	3 books	

1. How many books are there in F's shelf? _____

2. Which child has the least number of books and how many? _____

3. Which child has the maximum number of books and how many? _____

4. How many books are there in B's shelf? _____

5. If F puts all his books in the C's shelf, how many books will they have in all? _____

6. How many books did A and E have in all? _____

Answers

Numbers Beyond 1000
1. (a) 1003, 1005, 1006, 1007, 1009, 1012, 1013, 1014, 1016, 1017, 1018, 1019, 1022, 1024, 1025, 1026, 1028, 1029, 1030, 1031, 1033, 1034, 1035, 1037, 1038, 1040, 1041, 1042, 1043, 1045, 1046, 1047, 1049
   (b) 2082, 2083, 2085, 2086, 2087, 2088, 2089, 2091, 2093, 2094, 2095, 2096, 2098, 2099, 2102, 2103, 2105, 2106, 2107, 2109, 2110, 2112, 2114, 2115, 2117, 2118, 2120, 2121, 2123, 2124, 2126, 2127, 2128, 2129
   (c) 9952, 9953, 9954, 9956, 9957, 9958, 9959, 9961, 9962, 9964, 9965, 9966, 9968, 9970, 9971, 9973, 9974, 9975, 9977, 9978, 9979, 9982, 9983, 9985, 9986, 9987, 9989, 9990, 9991, 9992, 9994, 9996, 9997, 9998, 9999.

Place Value and Face Value
1. (a) 600, 6 (b) 900, 9 (c) 3000, 3
   (d) 90, 9 (e) 7000, 7 (f) 300, 3
   (g) 5, 5 (h) 1000, 1 (i) 400, 4
   (j) 100, 1 (k) 90, 9 (l) 8000, 8
2. (a) 7432, 2347 (b) 9831, 1389
   (c) 6520, 2056 (d) 8420, 2048
   (e) 7651, 1567 (f) 9642, 2469
   (g) 8753, 3578

Expanded Form
1. (b) 3000 + 900 + 8
   (c) 1000 + 500 + 20 + 4
   (d) 6000 + 300 + 30
   (e) 4000 + 500 + 10 + 3
   (f) 9000 + 900 + 90 + 9
2. (b) 8 × 1000 + 4 × 10 + 7 × 1
   (c) 9 × 1000 + 5 × 100 + 5 × 10 + 1 × 1
   (d) 6 × 1000 + 3 × 100 + 8 × 10 + 2 × 1
   (e) 1 × 1000 + 4 × 100 + 9 × 10 + 9 × 1
   (f) 7 × 1000 + 1 × 100 + 7 × 1
   (g) 2 × 1000 + 9 × 100 + 6 × 10 + 5 × 1
   (h) 6 × 1000 + 8 × 100 + 3 × 10 + 4 × 1

Roman Numerals
1. (a) VII (b) II (c) VIII
   (d) III (e) V (f) IX
   (g) IV (h) I (i) VI
   (j) X (k) XX (l) L
   (m) XXIX (n) XV (o) XVIII
   (p) XII (q) XVI (r) XIII
   (s) LXX (t) LX (u) C
   (v) CCC (w) D (x) M
2. (a) 10 (b) 4 (c) 7
   (d) 3 (e) 9 (f) 5
   (g) 8 (h) 2 (i) 21
   (j) 14 (k) 30 (l) 15
   (m) 17 (n) 12 (o) 19
   (p) 18 (q) 35 (r) 60
   (s) 50 (t) 200 (u) 40
   (v) 500 (w) 700 (x) 1000
3. (f) X (g) XX (h) D
   (i) CC (j) D (k) DC
   (l) C (m) C (n) IX
   (o) XVIII (p) C (q) M
   (r) VII (s) V (t) XL

Ordering Numbers
1. (a) 1740, 2160, 3154, 4295
   (b) 1005, 1045, 1405, 1645
   (c) 634, 6142, 6213, 6342
   (d) 1634, 4509, 5204, 7842
   (e) 453, 924, 2908, 4976
2. (a) 8192, 7104, 4521, 1864
   (b) 6121, 2727, 812, 432
   (c) 6145, 5161, 4152, 3541
   (d) 2732, 1632, 732, 632
   (e) 9026, 6029, 2069, 629
4. Triangle: 1 (top), 17, 11, 7, 15, 5, 13, 9, 3
5. (a) 1000 (b) 999 (c) 1000
   (d) 3469 (e) C (f) 899
   (g) IX (h) 9 hundreds (i) 6
   (j) 27
6. 4626, 4628, 4630, 4632, 4634, 4636, 4638, 4640, 4642, 4244, 4246, 4248, 4250, 4252, 4254, 4256
7. 7411, 7413, 7415, 7417, 7419, 7421, 7423, 7425, 7427, 7429, 7431, 7433, 7435, 7437, 7439, 7441, 7443, 7445, 7447, 7449, 7451, 7453, 7455, 7457, 7459
8. (a) 3428, 3430 (b) 1985, 1987
   (c) 4199, 4201 (d) 5860, 5862
   (e) 2998, 3000 (f) 4600, 4602

Adding Numbers
A. 1. 2080 2. 3000 3. 4998
   4. 425 5. 173 6. 1
   7. 1 8. 5829 9. 1940
   10. 8420
B. 1. 548 2. 8855 3. 4603
   4. 6072 5. 297
C. 1. 25, 25 2. 50, 50
   3. 500, 500 4. 1000, 1000
   5. 350, 350 6. 4000, 4000
   7. 3000, 3000 8. 250, 250
   9. 5, 5 10. 4500, 4500
D. 1. 7994 2. 8438 3. 8792
   4. 7014 5. 9330 6. 8941
E. 1. 9174 people 2. 4482 km
   3. 9485 kg 4. $4378
   5. 4000 kg 6. 9073 m

Subtracting Numbers
A. 1. 4771 2. 4494 3. 3515
   4. 2306 5. 6775 6. 2200
   7. 5640 8. 3188 9. 697
   10. 2710
B. 1. 483 2. $140 3. 1280
   4. 56 5. 8999 6. 2212

Face the Challenge
A. 1. 4000 + 610
   2. 2900 − 100
   3. 290
   4. 800 and 200
   5. 375 + 608 = 675 + 308
   6. 1475, 275
   7. (a)

Solve the Puzzles
A.

3	+	5	=	8
+		+		+
15	+	15	=	30
=		=		=
18	+	20	=	38

20	+	18	=	38
+		+		+
12	+	12	=	24
=		=		=
32	+	30	=	62

B.
1. 72; 6, 12; 2, 3, 4
2. 45; 5, 9; 5, 1, 9
3. 24; 6, 4; 3, 2, 2
4. 80; 4, 20; 1, 4, 5

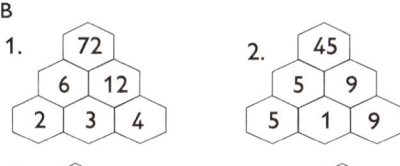
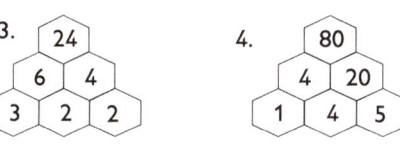

Rounding Off
A. 1. 60 2. 20 3. 80 4. 30
   5. 70 6. 40 7. 80 8. 70
   9. 30 10. 50 11. 40 12. 10
   13. 60 14. 80 15. 90
B. 1. 900 2. 200 3. 700 4. 400
   5. 800 6. 300 7. 200 8. 400

9. 500 10. 900 11. 200 12. 400
13. 3700 14. 4200 15. 7000 16. 7400
17. 1900 18. 8300
C. 1. 6000 2. 4000 3. 5000 4. 1000
5. 9000 6. 3000 7. 5000 8. 2000
9. 9000 10. 7000
D. 1. 480, 500   2. 920, 900
3. 1570, 1600   4. 270, 300
5. 850, 800   6. 670, 700

Multiplication
A. 1. 50 2. 60, 10 3. 180
4. 56 5. 100, 10 6. 1640
7. 100 8. 100, 4
B. 1. 846 2. 1320 3. 628
4. 1074
C. 1. 88 hats   2. 168 pages
3. 288 cherries 4. 228 strings
5. $750   6. 392 legs

Division
A. 1. 46 2. 9 3. 10, 5 4. 5, 1
5. 50 6. 4 7. 90 8. 10
9. 87 10. 430
B. 1. Q = 9, R = 0   2. Q = 18, R = 0
3. Q = 24, R = 2   4. Q = 12, R = 0
5. Q = 25, R = 0   6. Q = 12, R = 0
7. Q = 15, R = 1   8. Q = 9, R = 3

More Than, Less Than
A. 1. 84 2. 63 3. 35 4. 122
5. 197 6. 210 7. 21 8. 80
9. 18 10. 60 11. 12 12. 51
13. 75 14. 1
B. 1. 1598, 1698   2. 7344, 7444
3. 4210, 4310   4. 7468, 7568
5. 1932, 2032   6. 5501, 5601
7. 3676, 3776
C. 1. 5785, 6785   2. 1440, 2400
3. 4988, 5988   4. 6731, 7731
5. 2160, 3160   6. 8000, 9000
7. 4258, 5258

Fractions
A.
1.  2.  3.
4. 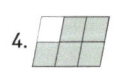 5. 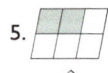 6.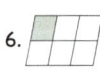
7.  8.  9.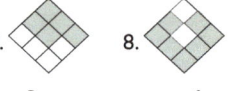

B. 1. $\frac{3}{6}$ 2. $\frac{4}{8}$
3. $\frac{5}{5}$ 4. $\frac{2}{5}$

Equivalent Fractions
A. 1. a. $\frac{1}{2}$ b. $\frac{2}{4}$ c. $\frac{3}{6}$
2. a. $\frac{1}{3}$ b. $\frac{3}{9}$ c. $\frac{2}{6}$
3. a. $\frac{1}{2}$ b. $\frac{2}{4}$ c. $\frac{3}{6}$
4. a. $\frac{1}{3}$ b. $\frac{2}{6}$ c. $\frac{3}{9}$

Ordering Fractions
A. 1. $\frac{7}{9} > \frac{6}{9} > \frac{5}{9} > \frac{4}{9} > \frac{3}{9} > \frac{1}{9}$
2. $\frac{1}{7} < \frac{2}{7} < \frac{4}{7} < \frac{5}{7} < \frac{6}{7} < \frac{7}{7}$
3. $1 > \frac{5}{6} > \frac{4}{6} > \frac{3}{6} > \frac{2}{6} > \frac{1}{6}$
4. $\frac{2}{8} < \frac{3}{8} < \frac{4}{8} < \frac{5}{8} < \frac{6}{8} < \frac{7}{8}$
5. $\frac{11}{12} > \frac{9}{12} > \frac{7}{12} > \frac{5}{12} > \frac{3}{12} > \frac{1}{12}$

Adding Fractions
A. 2. $\frac{4}{5}$ 3. $\frac{4}{6}$ 4. $\frac{4}{4}$ 5. $\frac{6}{9}$

Measuring Length
A. 1. 100 2. 400 3. 700 4. 300
5. 900 6. 800 7. 1200 8. 600
9. 1500 10. 500
B. 1. 1 2. 3 3. 8 4. 2
5. 11 6. 6 7. 7 8. 14
9. 1000 10. 9000 11. 7000 12. 3000
C. 1. 605 2. 220 3. 910 4. 508
5. 1212 6. 342 7. 888 8. 156
9. 1568 10. 1038
D. 1. b 2. a 3. c 4. a 5. b
E. 1. 99 m 1 cm
2. 61 m 70 cm
3. 49 m 85 cm
4. 52 km 81 m
5. 79 km 102 m
6. 17 km 36m
F. 1. 1000, 500   2. 1000, 500
3. 5000, 1000   4. 1000, 100
5. 1000, 600   6. 1000, 800
7. 900, 600   8. 12,000, 10,000
9. 10,000, 5   10. 7000, 3
11. 1200, 2   12. 18000, 2
G. 1. kg 2. m 3. l 4. l 5. kg
6. m 7. km 8. kg
H. 1. red ribbon, 16 m 2. 26 l 500 ml
3. 436 cm   4. 117 cm
5. 1000 ml   6. 6240 gm

Money
A. 1. 100 2. 800 3. 300
4. 615 5. 1025 6. 500
B. 1. Thirteen dollars fifty cents
2. Ten dollars
3. Forty one dollars twenty five cents
4. Ninety nine cents
5. Eight dollars eighteen cents
C. 1. 345 cents 2. $3.60 3. $56.31
4. $110.25 5. cents 6. $105

D. 1. $509.36 2. $748 3. $276.50
4. $78 5. $1480

Geometry
A. 1. one 2. no 3. two
4. point 5. definite 6. ray
D. 1. e 2. c 3. d 4. a 5. b
E. 1. Triangle 2. Hexagon 3. Square
4. Pentagon
F. 1. vertex 2. congruent
3. open 4. closed
5. flat, curved

Calender
A. 1. March 17, 2008
2. December 25, 2003
3. July 4, 2015
4. February 29, 2000
5. August 13, 2002
B. 1. 05-09-2016   2. 29-03-2001
3. 31-08-2014   4. 18-02-2005
5. 12-01-2009
C. 1. twelve   2. leap
3. 366   4. February
5. August   6. 52

Time
B. 1. 8:30 am 2. 5:15 pm 3. 12:38 pm
4. 11:45 pm 5. 6:21 am 6. 6:12 pm
C. 1. 120 minutes 2. 420 minutes
3. 75 minutes 4. 60 minutes
5. 300 minutes 6. 210 minutes
D. 1. 24 hours 2. 120 hours
3. 54 hours 4. 1 hour
5. 168 hours 6. 99 hours
E. 1. midnight 2. noon
3. minute hand 4. hour hand
5. half past ten 6. 7:00 am
7. 24 8. 60
9. minutes 10. hours

Data Handling
A. 1. Blue 2. Grey
3. Orange, White
B. 1. 18 books 2. G, 6 books
3. D, 20 books 4. 8 books
5. 30 books 6. 22 books

www.ingramcontent.com/pod-product-compliance
Lightning Source LLC
Chambersburg PA
CBHW040056160426
43192CB00002B/84